THE COMEDY BIBLE WORKBOOK

The Interactive Companion to "The New Comedy Bible"

BY JUDY CARTER

- 48 new exercises to turn problems into punchlines
- Build 60 minutes of original & authentic material
- Laugh Per Minute (LPM) system helps hone your material
- Daily jump starters to conquer procrastination
- Sections for capturing ideas and writing "Morning Writings"

> Judy Carter's workshop gave me the skills to have a successful career in stand-up comedy.
> – Maz Jobrani

The Comedy Bible Workbook

Note: this journal is available in print and as an interactive PDF compatible with PC, Mac, iOS, and Android devices. More information at https://thecomedybible.com/

Copyright © 2020 by Judy Carter

All rights reserved.
Printed in the United States of America.

No part of this publication may be reproduced or distributed in any form or by any means without the prior permission of the publisher. Requests for permission should be directed to: info@judycarter.com.

Neither the publisher nor the author is engaged in rendering legal, tax or other professional services through this book. The information is for business education purposes only. If expert assistance is required, the services of appropriate professionals should be sought. The publisher and the author shall have neither liability nor responsibility to any person or entity with respect to any loss or damage caused directly or indirectly by the information in this publication.

ISBN-10: 978-0-578-62212-5

Cover design by Joni McPherson, mcphersongraphics.com

Edited by Alan Roberts

TheComedyBible.com

Other Books by Judy Carter

Stand-up Comedy: The Book (Dell Publishing)

The Homo Handbook (Simon and Schuster)

The Comedy Bible (Simon and Schuster)

The Message of You: Turn Your Life Story into a Money-Making Speaking Career (St. Martin's Press)

The Message of You Journal: Finding Extraordinary Stories in an Ordinary Day (Comedy Workshops Publishing)

The New Comedy Bible (Indie Books International)

TABLE OF CONTENTS

Introduction
    How to Use this Workbook ix

Section 1: Exercises 1
👥 = Exercise with Comedy Buddy

    Exercise 1:   Where Are You on the Funny Scale? 3
    Exercise 2:   Commit to Your Comedy Vision 6
    Exercise 3:   Setting Up Your Comedy Bible Workbook 8
    Exercise 4:   Morning Writings - Waking & Creating 8
    Exercise 5:   Getting a Gig 8
    Exercise 6:   From Stage Fright to Savers 9
    Exercise 7:   Finding Your Comedy Buddy 👥 9
    Exercise 8:   Finding Your Authentic Topics 10
    Exercise 9:   Picking Your Best 3 Topics 11
    Exercise 10:   Mind Mapping Your Best 3 Topics 12
    Exercise 11:   Ranting and Raving to Laughs 👥 18
    Exercise 12:   Adding Act-Outs to Your Jokes 👥 18
    Exercise 13:   Organizing Your Jokes in Progress 18
    Exercise 14:   Adding Space Work to Your Act-Outs 👥 19
    Exercise 15:   Turn a Joke with a List of 3 19
    Exercise 16:   Writing Turns for Your Topics 21
    Exercise 17:   Creating Turns Starting with the Punchline ... 22
    Exercise 18:   Practice Mix Session 23
    Exercise 19:   Mixes – Finding Funny in Your Family 👥 23
    Exercise 20:   Expanding Your Material with Mixes 👥 24
    Exercise 21:   Researching Pro Comics 26
    Exercise 22:   Premises – Turning Unfunny to Funny 👥 27
    Exercise 23:   Reworking Your Setups 👥 28
    Exercise 24:   Adding Tags and Segues 👥 28
    Exercise 25:   Review and Rewrite Your Material 👥 29
    Exercise 26:   Creating a Killer Opening 👥 29
    Exercise 27:   Adding Callbacks to Close Strong 👥 30
    Exercise 28:   Get On Your Feet – Set List Fun 👥 32
    Exercise 29:   Organizing Your Set List 👥 33
    Exercise 30:   How to Memorize Your Act 33
    Exercise 31:   Exploring Your Comedy Persona 33
    Exercise 32:   Crowd Work 35
    Exercise 33:   Heckler Preparedness 👥 35
    Exercise 34:   Coming in on Time 👥 36
    Exercise 35:   Act Review - Calculating Your Laugh Score ... 36

Exercise 36:	Act Review – Rewriting Your Act	36
Exercise 37:	Bombing Savers	36
Exercise 38:	Self-Mocking Opening	37
Exercise 39:	Half and Half Mash-Ups	38
Exercise 40:	Comparison Jokes	39
Exercise 41:	Create a Dialogue Joke	41
Exercise 42:	Creating Political and Current Event Jokes 👥	42
Exercise 43:	Adding Impressions to Your Act	43
Exercise 44:	Creating Observational Jokes 👥	44
Exercise 45:	Riffing Onstage	45
Exercise 46:	Reluctant Admission	45
Exercise 47:	Terminology Twists	48
Exercise 48:	Annoying Acronyms	49

Section 2: Jokes in Progress by Topic 51
   Introduction 51
   Topic 1 52
   Topic 2 57
   Topic 3 62
   Topic 4 68
   Topic 5 73
   Topic 6 76
   Topic 7 81
   Topic 8 86
   Topic 9 91
   Topic 10 94

Section 3: My Act: Polished Jokes by Topic 99
   Introduction 99
   Topic 1 101
   Topic 2 104
   Topic 3 107
   Topic 4 110
   Topic 5 113
   Topic 6 116
   Topic 7 119
   Topic 8 122
   Topic 9 125
   Topic 10 128

Section 4: Set Lists 131
   Introduction 131
   3 Minute Set 132
   5 Minute Set 133
   10 Minute Set 134
   15 Minute Set 135
   30 Minute Set 136
   60 Minute Set 138
   Clean Set 141
   Themed Events (Women, Late Night, Charity Benefit, Gay Audience, etc.) 142

SECTION 5: Morning Writings 145
   Morning Writings: 31 Days Without Breaking the Chain 146
   Transcriptions from Your recorder ....
   About Judy Carter ....

How to Use This Workbook

You hold in your hands the recipient of *all* your ideas, good and bad, brilliant and stupid. Write down everything, because sometimes even the most idiotic ideas lead to polished gems.

Suggestions:

1. Register at TheComedyBible.com for updates and interactive help.

2. When doing the exercises in this workbook, refer to *The New Comedy Bible* for directions.

3. Each morning write for at least 10 minutes in your "Morning Writings." You can also use this time to transcribe your recorded audio off your phone from the day before.

4. Do at least one exercise a day.

5. As your jokes take form, copy and paste, or rewrite them, into the "Jokes in Progress" section of this workbook according to topic.

6. When your "Jokes in Progress" are ready to be performed, transfer them to the "My Act" section of this workbook.

7. If you have the printed workbook, put a sticky note on the edge of each section so you can easily find it. If you're using the PDF version, click the hyperlinks to go to each section.

The Comedy Bible Workbook **is available in print, or in an interactive PDF version which works on all PC, Mac, iOS and Android devices.**

Instructions for the PDF Version of this Book

After you download this version, use Abode Reader to view the PDF. If you don't have Adobe Reader, you can download for free at Adobe.com.

Then SAVE AS to your computer.

Make sure you work on this document when it's opened in Adobe Reader as it will NOT save when viewed in your browser.

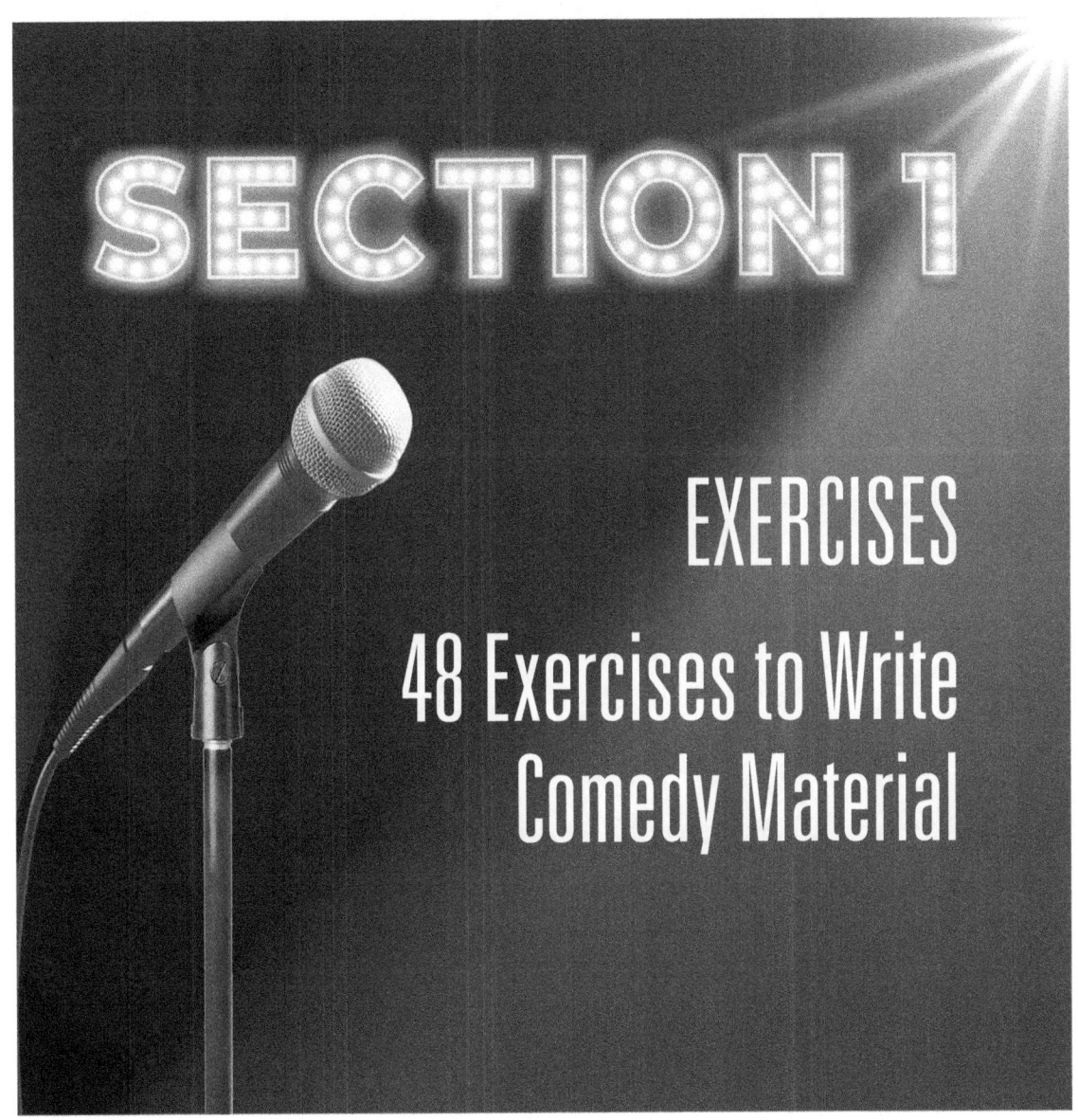

Please refer to *The New Comedy Bible* for instructions on each exercise.

EXERCISE 1: Where Are You on the Funny Scale?

1. **List of 3 Punchlines (Turns):** Write a punchline to this setup: *Three things will survive a nuclear bomb: venereal disease, cockroaches, and...*

    LIST 3 FUNNY ANSWERS.

    a. _____

    b. _____

    c. _____

2. **Writing Captions**

    Write 2 funny captions for this picture...

    a. _____

    b. _____

3. **Dialoguing Funny (Act-Outs):** Your mom says, "You're going out in that?!"
   WRITE 2 WITTY RESPONSES.

   1. _____
      _____
   2. _____
      _____

4. **Stand-up (Mixes):** Finish this setup: An ink pen is like sex because...
   LIST 5 EXAMPLES.

   1. _____
   2. _____
   3. _____
   4. _____
   5. _____

5. **Self-Mocking (Contrary Thinking):** *"I'm chubby, but there are some advantages to being overweight..."*
   LIST 3 FUNNY ADVANTAGES TO BEING OVERWEIGHT.

   1. _____
   2. _____
   3. _____

6. **Acronym Jokes (One-Liners):** *KFC, CPA, and VIP actually stand for...*
   WRITE OUT FUNNY DEFINITIONS FOR THESE ACRONYMS.

   KFC _____
   CPA _____
   VIP _____

   MAKE UP ONE OF YOUR OWN.

   _____

7. **Political Humor (Comparison Jokes):** *"My mother and the leader of our country have something in common, they both..."*

   WRITE TWO FUNNY RESPONSES.

   1. _____
   _____
   _____

   2. _____
   _____
   _____

8. **Family Jokes:** *"The weird thing about my father is..."*

   WRITE 2 FUNNY THINGS.

   1. _____
   _____
   _____

   2. _____
   _____
   _____

9. **Religious Jokes:** *"Last night, God gave me advice. S/he said..."*

   ACT OUT GOD GIVING YOU ADVICE.

   _____
   _____
   _____
   _____
   _____
   _____
   _____

10. **Sex Jokes** *"Is it me or is it really unattractive when you're in bed with someone and they say...?"*

    WRITE 2 FUNNY RESPONSES.

    1. _____
       _____
       _____
       _____

    2. _____
       _____
       _____
       _____

Your Funny Test Results

How many jokes/responses did you write? _____

Review this section in The New Comedy Bible to see where you land on the "Funny Scale."

Want to post your best answers? Go to TheComedyBible.com to learn how.

EXERCISE 2: Commit to Your Comedy Vision

1. **Visualize this...**

Close your eyes and visualize having the comedy career you want. Imagine yourself becoming successful.

- What does success look like?_____
  _____
  _____
  _____

- How do you feel? _____
  _____
  _____
  _____

- Who's around you? _____
  _____
  _____
  _____

- What are your most private thoughts at your moment of success?
  _____
  _____
  _____
  _____

2. Spend 10 minutes writing your success vision.

_____
_____
_____
_____
_____
_____
_____
_____
_____
_____
_____
_____

3. Write a goal you will achieve *one year* from now.
_____
_____
_____

4. Write that goal in your calendar *one year* from today.
_____
_____
_____
_____

5. **Make a Commitment!**

Don't keep your success plan a secret! Go to TheComedyBible.com and fill out a commitment form! You'll receive a motivational message to help you attain your goals. (Just return my phone calls when you get famous:)

EXERCISE 3: Setting Up Your Comedy Bible Workbook

While going through the print version of this workbook, place sticky notes at each section so you can quickly access them.

EXERCISE 4: Morning Writings – Waking & Creating

Before your coffee, write! Write everything down, including your observations, thoughts, and dreams. This is not high art, but a way to a clearer mind, better ideas and less anxiety. Begin now!

EXERCISE 5: Getting a Gig

Search Google to find open mics in your area.

Date and time of your 1st performance: _____

Location: _____

How many minutes will you do? _____

EXERCISE 6: Stage Fright to Savers

Write your top 3 fears related to performing.

1. _____
2. _____
3. _____

Visualize the fear happening, then write 3 savers for when you forget your act.

1. _____
2. _____
3. _____

EXERCISE 7: Finding Your Comedy Buddy

1. Post on the social pages at TheComedyBible.com and post a description of the kind of buddy you'd like to work with.
2. In the table below, create a list including names, phone numbers, and email addresses of those who might make good comedy buddies.
3. The results of your communication with each of them.
4. The date(s) you'll get together in person or on video chat with each person, and the results of each meeting.
5. Make sure you both have gigs on your calendars.

Name	Result of Comm.	Meeting Date

EXERCISE 8: Finding Your Authentic Topics

Jobs: List some jobs you've had or currently have.

1. _____
2. _____
3. _____
4. _____
5. _____

Life Stages: List the stages of life that apply to you now (See list in *The New Comedy Bible*).

1. _____
2. _____
3. _____
4. _____
5. _____

Relationship Status: What's your relationship status? (See list in *The New Comedy Bible*.)

_____
_____
_____
_____
_____

Minority Groups: Write a list of any minority or misunderstood group(s) you belong to.

1. _____
2. _____
3. _____
4. _____
5. _____

Upbringing: Write 5 things that were unusual about your upbringing.

1. _____
2. _____
3. _____
4. _____
5. _____

Fish out of water: Write in some noticeable ways in which you are a "Fish out of water."

1. _____
2. _____
3. _____
4. _____
5. _____

Heritage: List your religion, ethnicity, and/or your nationality.

1. _____
2. _____
3. _____

EXERCISE 9: Picking Your Best 3 Topics

1. _____
2. _____
3. _____

Look through your Morning Writings and see if you've already started writing about the topics above. Maybe a joke is there already. Move anything funny from your rantings, as well as these 3 main topics "Jokes in Progress" section of the book.

EXERCISE 10: Mind Mapping Your Best 3 Topics

Topic 1:	Topic 2:	Topic 3:
Sub-topic 1:	Sub-topic 1:	Sub-topic 1:
Sub-topic 2:	Sub-topic 2:	Sub-topic 2:
Sub-topic 3:	Sub-topic 3:	Sub-topic 3:
Sub-topic 4:	Sub-topic 4:	Sub-topic 4:
Sub-topic 5:	Sub-topic 5:	Sub-topic 5:

Enter your "Best 3 Topics" in the table below. Then under each one list 5 sub-topics (hard, weird, scary, stupid). Now create 3 separate mind maps in the balloons in this section. (See *The New Comedy Bible* for directions).

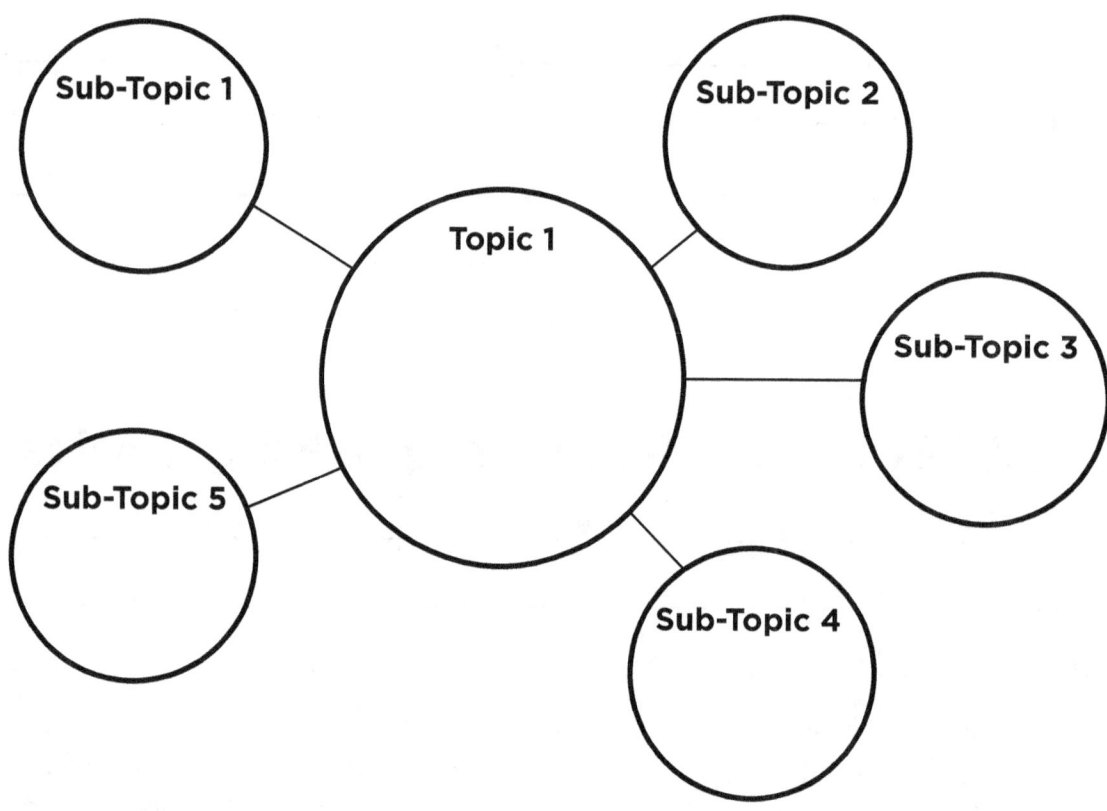

12 | THE COMEDY BIBLE WORKBOOK

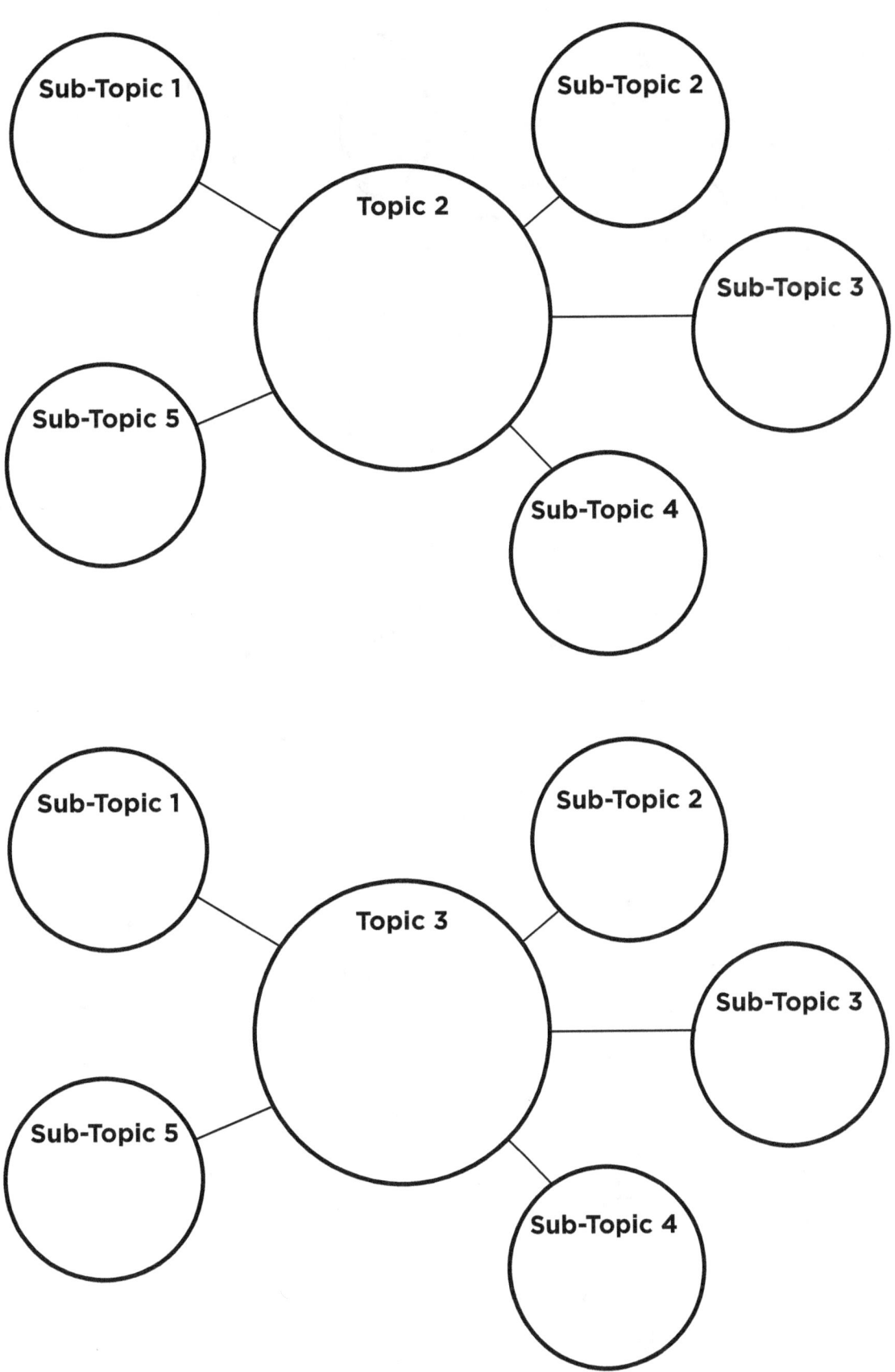

EXERCISES | 13

Mind Map

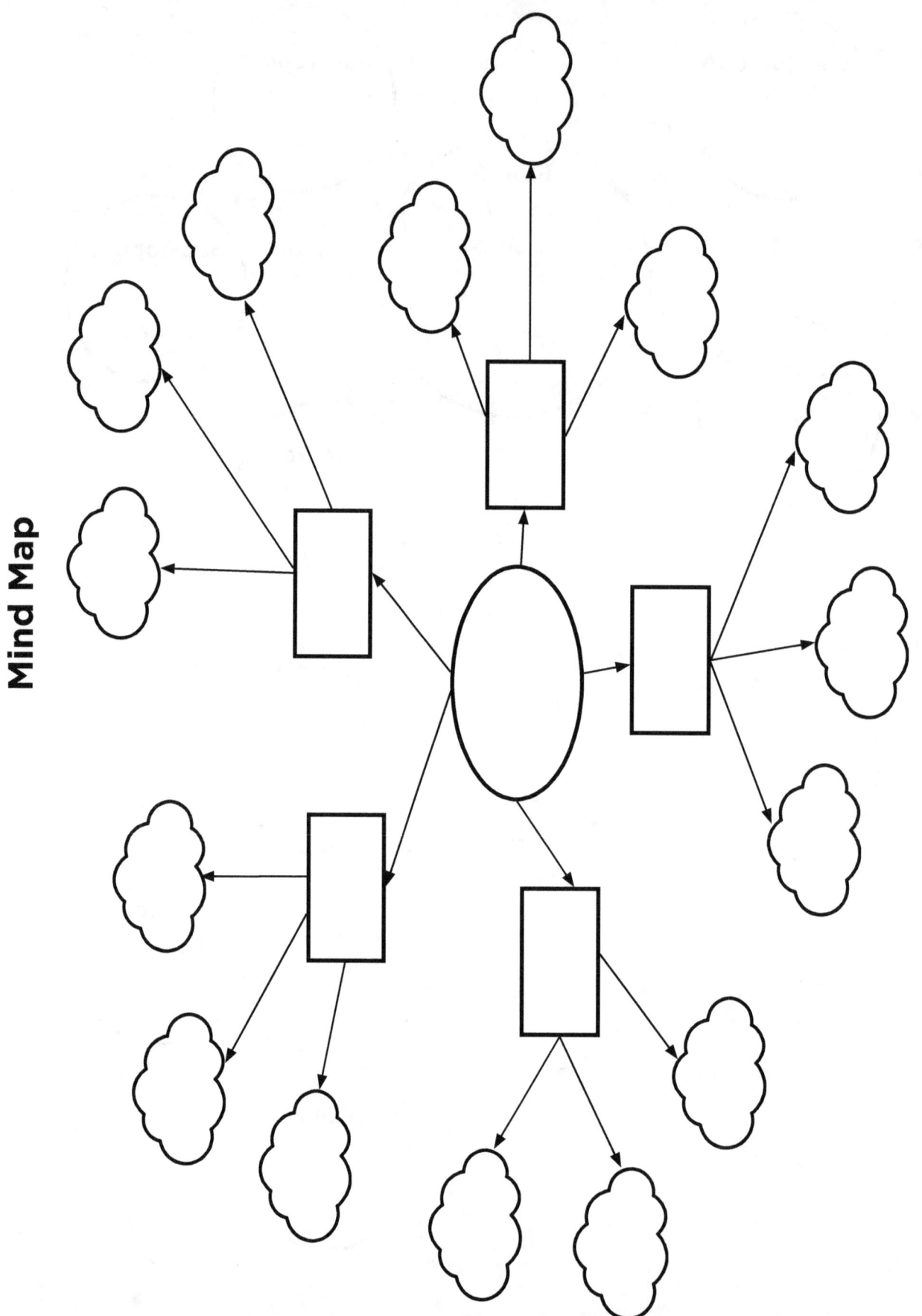

Mind Map

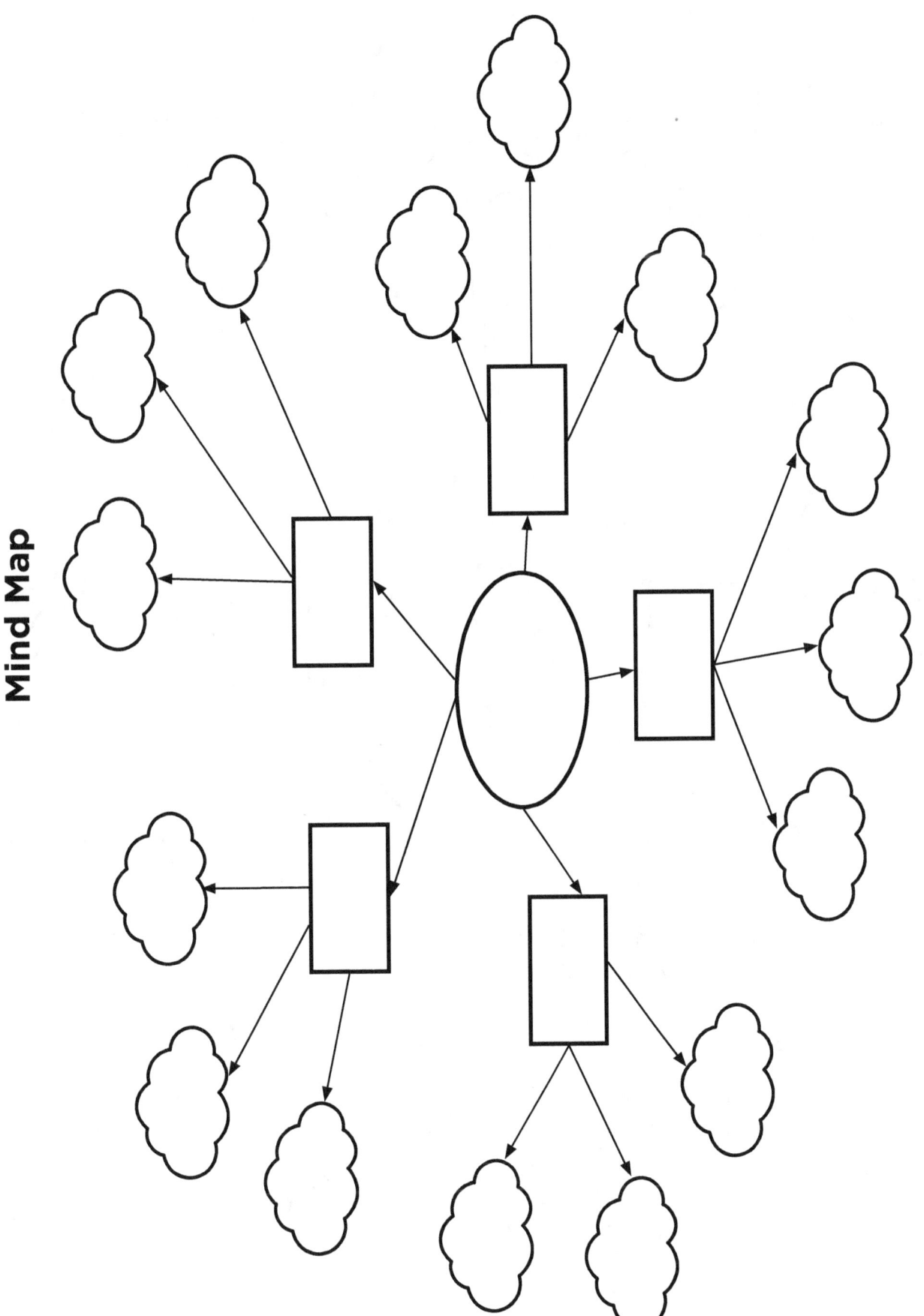

Mind Map

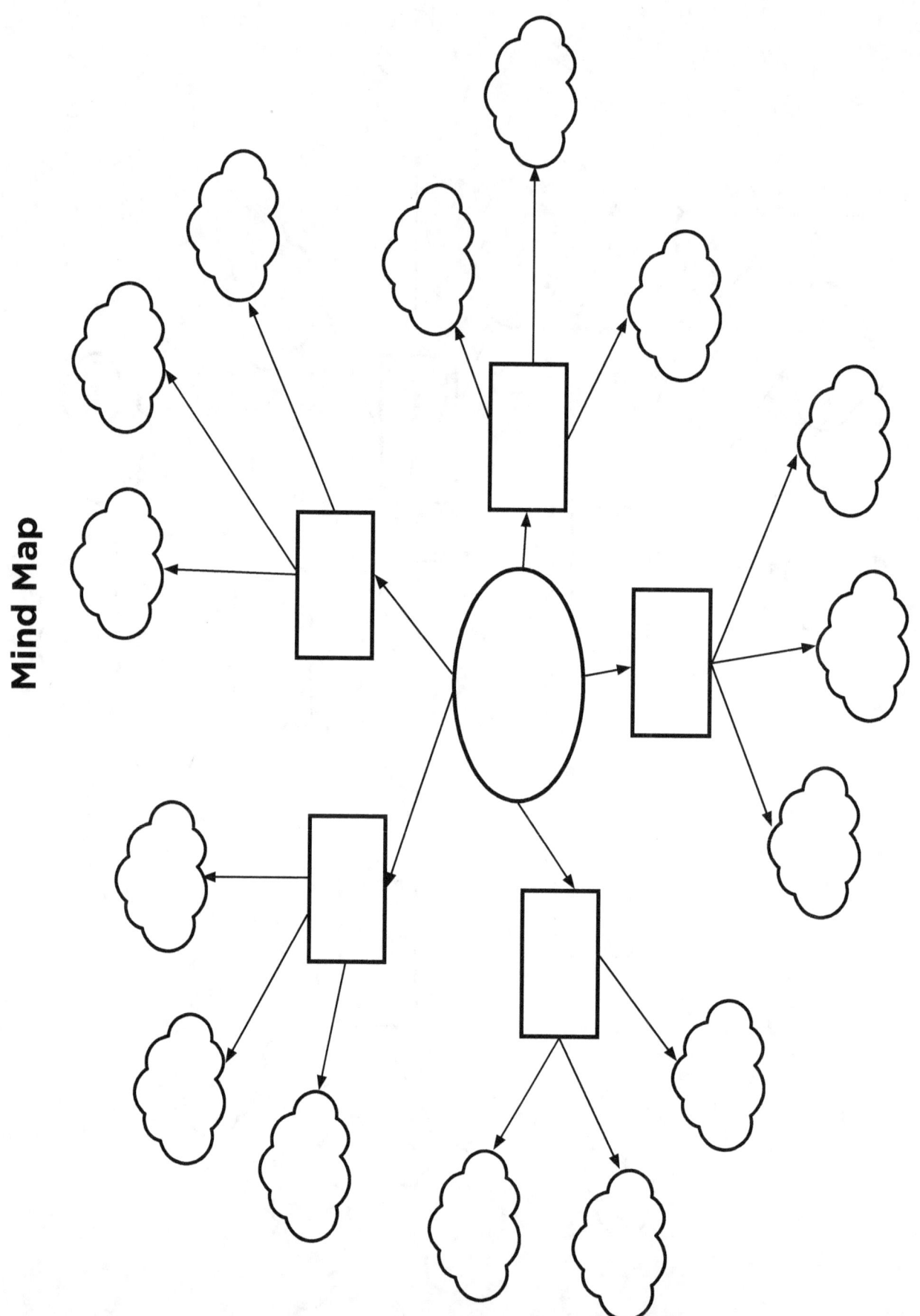

Mind Map

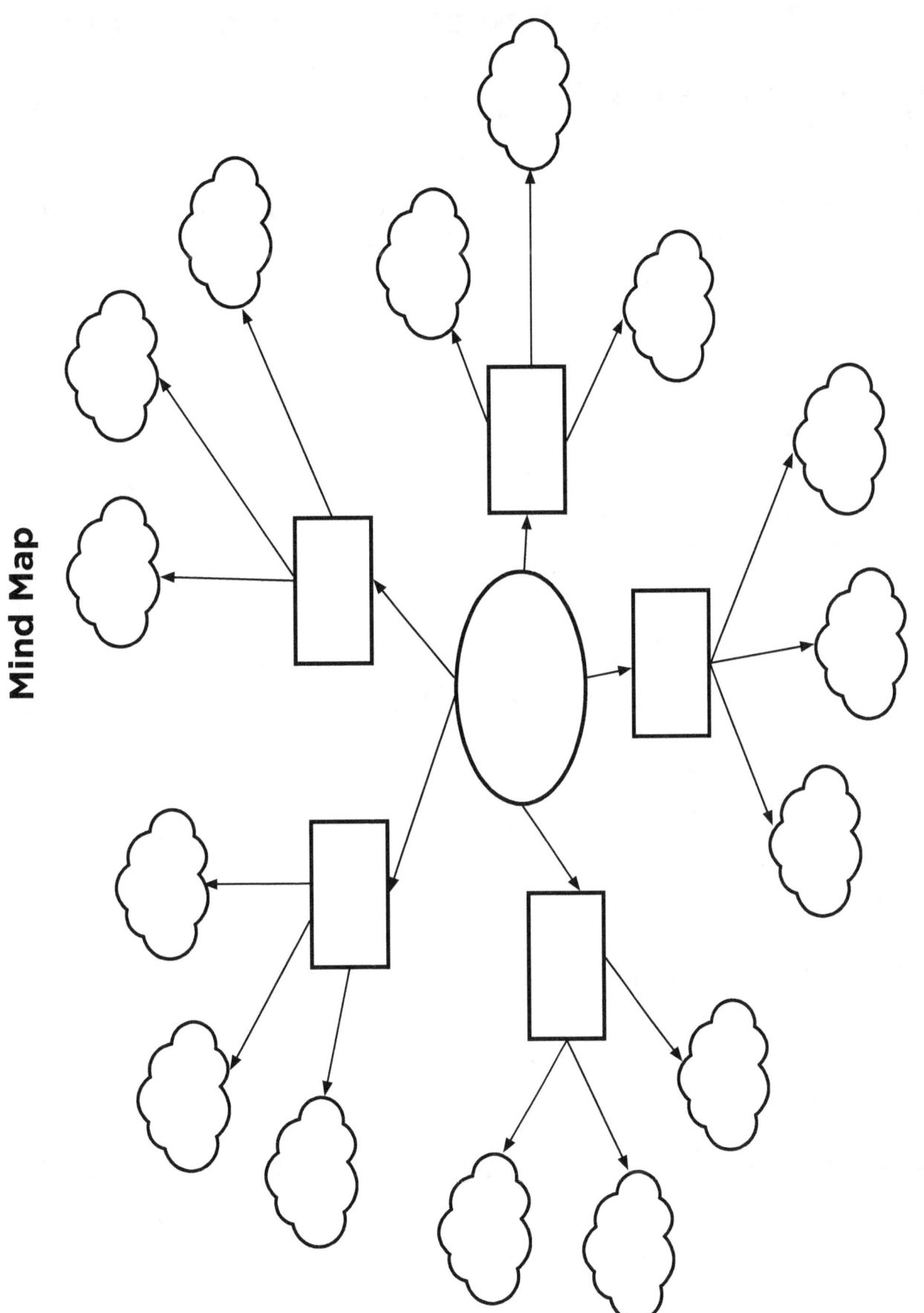

EXERCISE 11: Ranting and Raving to Laughs

Comedy Buddy Exercise

Give your buddy your main topic, sub-topic, and micro-topic outline.

With your buddy sitting and you standing, have them randomly pick one of your topics, then set a timer and RANT FOR ONE MINUTE on it by saying...

- Topic/Sub-topic is HARD, because...
- Topic/Sub-topic is WEIRD, because...
- Topic/Sub-topic is SCARY, because...
- Topic/Sub-topic is STUPID, because...

You can also do this by asking, "You know what's WEIRD about (INSERT YOUR TOPIC)...?" Add any material you come up with to "Jokes in Progress by Topic" section of this workbook. You should have ten-to-thirty fledging jokes.

EXERCISE 12: Adding Act-Outs to Your Jokes in Progress

Comedy Buddy Exercise

Do the Act-Out Practice Session 1 and 2 in *The New Comedy Bible.* Then try to drive all the topics in your mind map to an Act-Out.

 As your rants turn into jokes, copy them to the "Jokes in Progress by Topic." While working on these jokes, transfer them to your "My Act" folder.

EXERCISE 13: Organizing Your Jokes in Progress

Move some of your working material from "Morning Writings" and "My Exercises" folders to the "Jokes in Progress by Topic" section of this workbook.

EXERCISE 14: Adding Space Work to Your Act-Outs

Comedy Buddy Exercise

Using the jokes in the "Jokes in Progress by Topic" folder, rehearse your space work until it becomes second nature. You want to be able to speak while acting out mini-scenes. Try your act-outs over and over with your Comedy Buddy until they feel comfortable.

EXERCISE 15: Turn a Joke with a List of 3

Practice writing a List of 3 by finishing this setup:

"Relationships are HARD. There are 3 SUBTLE clues your relationship's over:

He's not listening when you talk…

You're not going out to dinner very often…

And…"

What's a super obvious clue that you've broken up?

_____

Now, rewrite it, and make it even more obvious. (See examples in *The New Comedy Bible*).

_____

_____

Then make it even MORE obvious and extreme.

_____

_____

Create multiple List of 3s on the topic of DEAD-END JOBS.

Work is HARD. There are 3 SUBTLE clues you're in a dead-end job:

Small/Subtle _____

Small/Subtle _____

Big/Obvious _____

 **Submit your answers at TheComedyBible.com for feedback, and check out the work of other aspiring comedians.**

List of 3: OBVIOUS-OBVIOUS-WEIRD

Now practice with a different List of 3: **Obvious-Obvious-Weird.**

"It's scary how being broke creeps up on you. There are three signs you're broke..."

Write two unfunny (obvious) signs that you're broke (because the setup is always unfunny).

1. _____
2. _____

In this next section, use **Obvious-Obvious-Weird**.

Here's your setup:

"It's scary to realize you have an addiction. You know it's time to stop drinking when..."

Make the first two small or subtle. Don't try to be funny; just write down subtle signs that make you wonder if it's time to stop drinking.

1. _____
2. _____

Now, for the third reason, let your mind go and come up with an extreme and obvious reason why you need to stop drinking. Then, ratchet that up a few notches to WEIRD. Write as many as possible below:

3. _____
_____
_____
_____
_____

Did you write something like this?

"When you wake up in the morning, it's the middle of next week."

EXERCISE 16: Writing Turns for Your Topics

Add several different List of 3s from Exercises 8 & 9's "Your Topics." For example, if one of your topics is "Being raised by religious fanatics," create a setup such as: "It's HARD being raised by religious zealots. There are three subtle clues your parents are too religious..."

Write two subtle things, then a third crazy/weird clue that your parents are overly religious. Try to follow it with an act-out.

Write the Setup

YOUR TOPIC is (weird, hard, scary stupid). There are 3 subtle clues that (INSERT YOUR TOPIC)...

Setup: _____

Clue 1: (subtle) _____

Clue 2: (subtle) _____

Clue 3: (obvious) _____

Repeat for 2 other topics:

Setup 2: _____

Clue 1: (subtle) _____

Clue 2: (subtle) _____

Clue 3: (obvious) _____

Setup 3: _____

Clue 1: (subtle) _____

Clue 2: (subtle) _____

Clue 3: (obvious) _____

Now, write a turn starting with this punchline: *"I divorced my husband/wife!"*

SETUP: _____

_____

PAYOFF: *"I divorced my husband/wife!"*

 Copy and paste at least 3 of your List of 3s into your "Jokes in Progress by Topic" folder, in the document with the correct topic.

EXERCISE 17: Creating Turns Starting with the Punchline

Look through your Jokes in Progress by Topic, or your ranting and ravings. What information do you give the audience in the beginning of a joke? Such as:

"I'm happy to be here!"

This is something comics say all the time, but Jim Jeffries makes it a punchline.

"I now have a child... so boy am I happy to be here!"

Write the info you want to give the audience here:

I just lost weight, I'm single, I'm from Arkansas...

Information to give the audience:

1. _____
2. _____
3. _____

Write 5 different lead-ins to make the information funny.

For instance, *"I'll be going slow tonight...I'm from Arkansas!"*

1. _____
2. _____
3. _____
4. _____
5. _____

 From this point on, move any material that works from your IDEA or EXERCISE Section to your "Jokes in Progress by Topic" Section.

EXERCISE 18: Practice Mix Session

In Exercise 1 you were given this line: *"A pen is just like sex because ..."*

Write 10 comparisons of pens to sex.

1. _____
2. _____
3. _____
4. _____
5. _____
6. _____
7. _____
8. _____
9. _____
10. _____

 Look through your Ideas folder. Can any of them inspire a mix? Give it a go and see if anything's worthy of transferring to your "Jokes in Progress by Topic" section, or even your "My Act" section containing more polished jokes.

EXERCISE 19: Mixes – Finding Funny in Your Family

Comedy Buddy Exercise

What follows is a solid method for writing jokes, with TURNS, about your family. Make sure everything you write is BASED ON TRUTH.

5-Step Mix Method

1. My (INSERT **FAMILY MEMBER,** e.g., Mom, Dad, Grandma)

2. INSERT ATTITUDE: Hard, weird, scary, or stupid. For instance, "Mom was SCARY..." "Grandpa was WEIRD..."

3. BECAUSE…s/he was often very (**INSERT DISTURBING QUALITY,** e.g., self-obsessed, overly helpful, angry, foul mouthed, bitter, fearful, confused).

4. DO AN EXAGGERATED ACT-OUT OF HER/HIM IN A SCENE, TALKING TO SOMEONE, ILLUSTRATING THEIR DISTURBING QUALITY. If your mother's very "angry," then put her in a scene exaggerating just how angry she is.

5. Say, "Can you imagine my (FAMILY MEMBER) as a (**INSERT UNLIKELY PROFESSION FOR SOMEONE WITH THAT DISTURBING QUALITY**)?" ACT-OUT THE MIX OF YOUR RELATIVE WITH THE DISTURBING QUALITY IN AN UNLIKELY PROFESSION.

 For more examples and directions, review this exercise in *The New Comedy Bible*.

1. My (Insert family member): _____
2. INSERT ATTITUDE (Hard, Weird, Scary, or Stupid): _____
3. BECAUSE… (Insert disturbing quality): _____
   _____
4. Do an exaggerated ACT-OUT of him/her in a scene, illustrating their disturbing quality: _____
   _____
5. Say, "Can you imagine my (Insert family member) as a (Insert unlikely profession for someone with that disturbing quality)?" ACT-OUT the Mix of your relative with the disturbing quality in the unlikely profession.

EXERCISE 20: Expanding Your Material with Mixes

 Comedy Buddy Exercise

Working with your Comedy Buddy, read your material out loud and, at the end of each joke, ask:

- "What if…"
- "That's just like…"
- "Can you imagine if…"

For a minimum of 30 minutes, work with your Comedy Buddy on adding mixes to your material. Remember, every joke doesn't have to have a mix. Consider yourself brilliant if you create 5 mixes out of 30 jokes. Write them below and transfer your favorites to the "Jokes in Progress by Topic" folder.

MIXES TO MY EXISTING TOPICS:

_____
_____
_____
_____
_____
_____
_____
_____
_____
_____
_____
_____
_____
_____
_____
_____
_____
_____
_____

 Your "Jokes in Progress by Topic" folder should be filling up with material. Now let's carve that material into a killer stand-up act and start transferring jokes to your "My Act > Polished Jokes by Topic" section of this workbook.

EXERCISE 21: Researching Pro Comics

Watch three minutes of one of the comics at TheComedyBible.com in the Exercise's section and answer these questions:

1. What are the topic and attitude? _____

2. What's the premise? _____

3. What's the payoff? _____

Watch 3 minutes of any comic on TheComedyBible.com and answer these questions:

1. How many laughs did the comic get in 3 minutes?

   Comic: _____ Laughs in 3 minutes: _____

2. How many laughs is that per minute? _____

3. How many seconds were there between laughs, on average? _____

Write out one of their jokes and answer the following: _____
_____

4. What was the setup?

   Comic: _____ Setup: _____
   _____

5. What was the attitude/emotion conveyed in the setup? "Hard," "Weird," "Scary," or "Stupid?" (Did they say it or imply it?) _____

6. What was the topic of the joke? _____

7. What was the premise of the joke? _____

8. On the payoff/laugh: Was there an act-out? Was a surprise/turn revealed?

   If yes, what was it? _____
   _____

9. Did the comic then do another joke on the same topic, building a "chunk" on that topic? If yes, what was it? _____
_____

26 | THE COMEDY BIBLE WORKBOOK

EXERCISE 22: Premises — Turning Unfunny to Funny

Comedy Buddy Exercise

For this exercise, let's use an unfunny topic: Funerals. With your Comedy Buddy, throw out different attitude words and come up with at least three insightful PREMISES for each of our four attitudes. (See examples in *The New Comedy Bible*.)

1. Funerals are HARD because... (3 PREMISES)

    1a. _____

    1b. _____

    1c. _____

2. Funerals are WEIRD because... (3 PREMISES)

    2a. _____

    2b. _____

    2c. _____

3. Funerals are SCARY because... (3 PREMISES)

    3a. _____

    3b. _____

    3c. _____

4. Funerals are STUPID because... (3 PREMISES)

    4a. _____

    4b. _____

    4c. _____

Next, take your most promising funeral premises and drive them to an act-out or a turn. If your premise is solid, the act-out is easy! Put your best jokes in the "Jokes in Progress by Topic" section of this workbook.

EXERCISE 23: Reworking Your Setups

Comedy Buddy Exercise

Using all you've learned about premises, go back through your material and rewrite the setups of each joke in your "Jokes in Progress by Topic" folder, making sure your:

- Setups have ATTITUDE

- Targets DESERVE to be made fun of

- Setups make SENSE

- Background INFORMATION is no more than two sentences prior to getting into the joke

- Setups contain PRESENT TENSE verbs ("There I AM" rather than "There I WAS")

- Setups are as SHORT as possible

- Setups have a CLEAR premise

- Premises are something the audience hasn't heard before

EXERCISE 24: Adding Tags and Segues

Comedy Buddy Exercise

Go to the "My Act" section of this workbook. Practice delivering each of the jokes to your Comedy Buddy and add a TAG at the end of each one, repeating the ATTITUDE you used in the setup (hard, weird, scary, stupid). Before moving to your next joke using an Attitude Segue, your Comedy Buddy will encourage you to improvise new material on the spot. Perhaps another act-out, a turn, a comment—anything we've covered so far! You'll be surprised at the funny stuff living between your jokes. Only after you've exhausted all possibilities for more act-outs, another premise, or another turn, use attitude words to segue to the next joke. Push each other further and further, stretching those comedy muscles, because that's what it takes to be a pro.

EXERCISE 25: Review and Rewrite

 **Comedy Buddy Exercise**

With your Comedy Buddy, go through all the jokes in your "Jokes in Progress by Topic" section. For every joke you like enough to put in your act, run it through the 11 review steps below. Some of your jokes will die here, while some will "graduate" to your "My Act" Section.

Run every one of your jokes through these 11 qualifiers:

1. Does the target DESERVE to be made fun of?
2. Does your setup make SENSE?
3. Does your setup have ATTITUDE?
4. Is the setup as SHORT as possible?
5. Is your setup in the PRESENT TENSE?
6. Do any of your jokes include: "How are you doing?" "True story…"
7. Is any of your material inauthentic?
8. Does the joke include act-outs?
9. Does the joke go somewhere unexpected?
10. Does the joke have a clear premise (stated opinion)?
11. Do *you* like what you're saying?

EXERCISE 26: Creating a Killer Opening

 **Comedy Buddy Exercise**

Pick an Opening Joke

FOLLOWING THE GUIDELINES in the last section, go through all your jokes in "My Act" and "Jokes in Progress" and while you're at it, look through your morning writings and voice transcriptions and pick a few jokes to use as your opening. If you're unsure, that's OK, just choose a few as placeholders.

While standing in front of your Comedy Buddy, try these exercises.

1. Pick out a few jokes you think would make good openers. They should set the tone for your act. They can be jokes about yourself or about the audience.

2. Practice getting the audience to applaud two obvious things. Then practice sliding into your opening joke in an organic way.

3. Next, have your Comedy Buddy shout out some situations as you walk on the stage and react in the moment. For example:

    - Phone starts ringing
    - The comic before trashed women, and you're a woman
    - A waiter drops glasses
    - The entire front row gets up and leaves
    - The club is excessively warm
    - There's a drunken bachelorette party
    - The emcee mispronounces your name

4. After improvising a reaction, practice going into your first joke. If the transition doesn't feel natural, try out different jokes to open with.

5. Add your opener to the Set List Section of this workbook.

EXERCISE 27: Adding Callbacks to Close Strong

Comedy Buddy Exercise

Take a look at your material. Which jokes would you like to open with, or definitely include in the first few minutes of your set? What word, phrase or theme do you feel would be fun to repeat later or at the end of your set? Run through some callback ideas with your Comedy Buddy. (See *The New Comedy Bible* for examples.)

Opening Joke: _____

_____

_____

Word, Phrase or Theme to repeat later: _____

_____

Callback Ideas: _____
_____
_____
_____

Opening Joke: _____
_____
_____

Word, Phrase or Theme to repeat later: _____
_____

Callback Ideas: _____
_____
_____
_____

Opening Joke: _____
_____
_____

Word, Phrase or Theme to repeat later: _____
_____

Callback Ideas: _____
_____
_____
_____

EXERCISE 28: Get on Your Feet Set List Fun

Comedy Buddy Exercise

Let's practice being loose with an exercise many comedy clubs host as a show called "Set List — Comedy Without a Net."

Below is a sample SET LIST. Attack these topics with ATTITUDE. Then drive them to a premise (opinion or insight) and get to an ACT-OUT or a TURN.

Talk about *why* these topics are hard, weird, scary, or stupid.

- Shopping when you're broke
- Picking a tattoo
- Women's tennis
- Celebrity weddings
- Dating when you're older
- College cafeteria food
- Living in a dorm
- Eating vegan with friends who are meat eaters
- Being sober when your friends are drunk
- Donut holes
- Holidays with your family
- Dog sleeping in your bed
- Life coaches

When loose, you might find you're creating some killer bits in the moment. For that reason, record these sessions and transcribe any winners to your Morning Writings.

EXERCISE 29: Organizing Your Set List

Comedy Buddy Exercise

Organize your polished jokes into a set.

1. Create code words.
2. Organize your set list(s).
3. Edit your set list(s).
4. Know with certainty what your last bit is and its length.

Put your set lists in the "Set List" section of this workbook.

EXERCISE 30: How to Memorize Your Act

TAKE YOUR CHUNKS OUT FOR A WALK

Do this exercise according to instructions in *The New Comedy Bible*.

EXERCISE 31: Exploring Your Comedy Persona

Let's get in touch with what makes you unique, while learning how to expand on your distinctive characteristics.

Pick 2 or 3 of these describing you:

- ☐ Optimistic
- ☐ Mom-type
- ☐ Sarcastic
- ☐ Angry
- ☐ Shy
- ☐ Political
- ☐ Dark
- ☐ Rebel

- ☐ Nerd
- ☐ Loser
- ☐ Slacker
- ☐ Brown-noser
- ☐ Vulnerable
- ☐ Sexually obsessed
- ☐ Cutting-edge
- ☐ Neurotic

- ☐ Awkward
- ☐ Blunt
- ☐ Cheerleader
- ☐ Shy
- ☐ Geek
- ☐ Lazy
- ☐ Indecisive
- ☐ Prankster

1. Use the 2 or 3 characteristics from above to write new material. Ask yourself what's been hard/weird/scary/stupid about being (INSERT YOUR QUALITY)?

   Write some new material for these qualities. If nothing comes up, try a different attribute and/or attitude. Write any strong material below.

2. Look in your closet. What outfit reflects your persona?

EXERCISE 32: Crowd Working an Audience

After studying the various techniques on audience participation, mark a place in your Set List where you'll commit to improvising with the audience the next time you perform.

- First, determine if this particular audience is open to participating. Audiences form a personality, and some audiences, just like first dates, do NOT want to get involved.

- Have strong material to go into AFTER you improvise.

- If you still feel uncomfortable winging it, take an improv class to practice "Yes, and..." techniques, or join a local Toastmasters club, which is another great way to learn improv.

EXERCISE 33: Heckler Preparedness

Comedy Buddy Exercise

Practice your act while your Comedy Buddy heckles you according to instructions in *The New Comedy Bible*. Engage your buddy/heckler in a dialogue following this format:

1. Repeat the heckle – so the entire audience has heard it.

2. Ask the heckler a question – this gives you time to play with a response.

3. Respond with something funny.

Come up with 5 original comebacks and add them here.

1. _____
2. _____
3. _____
4. _____
5. _____

EXERCISE 34: Coming in on Time

Comedy Buddy Exercise

Practice timing your set. Understand that timing your rehearsal is very different from a club setting due to laughs and audience interaction. Rehearse segues to your last bit from various sections in your act.

EXERCISE 35: Act Review — Calculating Your Laugh Score

Listen to the recording of your act with your Set List in front of you. Write next to each joke a number from 0 to 5 using instructions in *The New Comedy Bible* as a reference.

1. Add up your total laughter points: _____

2. Minutes onstage: _____

3. Divide line 1 by line 2 and enter your LPM: _____

Calculate your results in *The New Comedy Bible*.

EXERCISE 36: Act Review — Rewriting Your Act

Review the jokes that got an LPM score of 1 or 2 and rewrite them in your "My Act" folder by answering the questions in *The New Comedy Bible*.

Rewrite, perform and repeat.

EXERCISE 37: Bombing Savers

In Exercise 6, you created some "Savers" to use when forgetting your act. Write at least 5 Bombing Savers below:

1. _____
2. _____
3. _____
4. _____
5. _____

Look through all the bombing suggestions and pick your favorites to do next time you're tanking:

1. _____
2. _____
3. _____
4. _____
5. _____

EXERCISE 38: Self-Mocking Opening

Referring to the instructions in *The New Comedy Bible*, write your most obvious imperfections.

My 5 OBVIOUS visuals about myself, or my character defects, are:

1. _____
2. _____
3. _____
4. _____
5. _____

Take each of those 5 defects through this simple Self-Mocking comedy method:

1. *"I'm..."* Insert something that's obvious or a little embarrassing about you.

   _____

2. Next, add a one-word comment, something like *"Whoo hoo!"*

3. In the next part of the joke, *explain* why you proclaimed *"Whoo hoo!"* by saying this line:

   "Hey! There are advantages to... (being bald, being fat, being negative, being insensitive.)" _____

4. Now come up with at least 5 reasons why it's a real bonus having your characteristic.

   a. _____
   b. _____

c. _____

d. _____

e. _____

5. If you're able to flow into an act-out on any of them, an even bigger laugh follows.

EXERCISE 39: Half and Half Mash-Ups

Revisit the list of topics you created in Exercise 7: My Authentic Topics.

Add to that list:

1. Your hobbies and interests

   _____

   _____

2. Places you've lived

   _____

   _____

3. Other interesting tidbits about you (hobbies, phobias, etc.)

   _____

   _____

Looking over the list, insert your personal information into these mash-up examples:

"I was born in (INSERT PLACE) *but I live in* (INSERT PLACE) *and that means ...*"

"*I had* (INSERT FORMER JOB) *and I've had* (INSERT ANOTHER FORMER JOB), *and that means...*"

I'm part (INSERT ETHNIC BACKGROUND) *and part* (ETHNIC BACKGROUND) *and that means, I* (INSERT MASH-UP)..."

Repeat this method at least 10 times with different topics and record your answers.

When finished, pick the funniest ones and record the clunkers in your "Jokes in Progress by Topic" section, and the winners in your "My Polished Jokes" section.

EXERCISE 40: COMPARISON JOKES

Comparison Joke: Them vs. Me

In this joke, compare yourself to someone more successful than you.

1. Pick a current celebrity or well-known figure and act out a recent quote or article that makes them sound successful.

2. Do an act-out comparing something similar in your life with the celebrity's.

Write two jokes using this formula:

(CELEBRITY) *says,* (INSERT ACT-OUT) _____. *That's so* (INSERT ATTITUDE) *because I'm* _____.

    a. _____

    _____

    _____

    b. _____

    _____

    _____

Comparison jokes also work with a TURN rather than an act-out.

Write two jokes using each of these formulas:

1. *It's HARD in this economy hearing about rich celebrity lifestyles.* (INSERT A CELEBRITY AND WHAT THEY HAVE) _____ . *OMG! I'd be lucky to...* _____.

    a. _____

    _____

    _____

    b. _____

    _____

    _____

2. It's SCARY hearing so many politicians getting away with corruption. (INSERT PUBLIC FIGURE AND WHAT THEY GOT AWAY WITH) _____. I'd be lucky to..._____.

   a. _____

   _____

   _____

   b. _____

   _____

   _____

3. It's WEIRD hearing about the stuff super-rich people do. (INSERT A RICH PERSON AND WHAT THEY DID)_____. I'd be lucky to..._____.

   a. _____

   _____

   _____

   b. _____

   _____

   _____

Comparison Jokes: BEFORE vs NOW

The simple Before vs. Now comparison works for sharing things you've noticed changing over the years.

Fill in the blanks below with at least 3 different versions of the Before vs Now method.

1. It's WEIRD how getting older changes what you want in a relationship. Before, I used to want _____

   (DO AN ACT-OUT) *and now I want* _____

   (DO AN ACT-OUT).

2. *The state of the economy has really changed my goals. Before, I used to...*

   _____

   (DO AN ACT-OUT). *Now I...*_____

   DO AN ACT-OUT).

3. *When I first started dating I was looking for* _____

   (DO AN ACT-OUT). *Now what I want is...*_____

   (DO AN ACT-OUT).

Comparison Jokes: My Culture/Home vs. Your Culture/Home

Fill in the blanks with at least 3 different versions.

1. *Moving is HARD because the gestures you use can be interpreted differently in a new place. In my hometown, we...*

   _____

   Here in (INSERT CITY), *you...* _____

2. *Traveling around the country/world, you notice how WEIRD some places are. Like in* (NAME OF CITY/TOWN)..._____

   But in (NAME OF THIS CITY)... _____

EXERCISE 41: CREATE A DIALOGUE JOKE

1. Make a list of 3 stupid things people have said to you, or stupid things you've heard celebrities say.

   a. _____

   b. _____

   c. _____

2. Come up with 3 funny retorts based on what you "wish you'd said," or what someone else should've said.

   a. _____

   b. _____

   c. _____

3. Look through your material to see if you can extend an existing joke by adding a Dialogue Joke.

___

EXERCISE 42: Creating Political and Current Event Jokes

👥 Comedy Buddy Exercise

Grab your Comedy Buddy, go online and find 3 current news stories. Then use these 3 formulas to jam new material.

1. Start a joke with something STUPID or WEIRD that the target of your joke refers to. Then come up with a retort someone should've said back to them.

    Example:

    *"Today, a conservative Christian Pastor said, 'I'm running for president of the U.S. because God told me to.' That's **WEIRD BECAUSE** God told me not to vote for him!"*

___

A fun exercise with your Comedy Buddy is to have one of you throw out something in the news while the other comes up with a funny retort.

2. Create a MIX joke by putting the target into a different situation, or by comparing your topic to something or someone else. These mixes usually start with:

   "Can you imagine if..."

   Or, *"It's like... "*

   _____
   _____
   _____
   _____

3. Futurize the joke by coming up with a MIX based on, *"Next thing you know..."* or, *"Can you imagine if...? It would be like..."*

   _____
   _____
   _____
   _____

4. Post your material on Twitter. It's the perfect destination for short lived political humor, and you just might get discovered! (Use #ComedyBible)

EXERCISE 43: Adding Impressions to your Act

1. Make a list of celebrity impressions you do.

2. Remove anyone who's deceased or no longer in the public consciousness.

3. Now, go back to the jokes you wrote in the Exercise 18: Practice Mix Session.

   Take one of your existing jokes and tag on an impression. Use lead-ins like: *"What if..."* and *"That's just like..."*

4. Revisit your jokes from Exercise 19: Family Jokes Using Mixes. See if you can add a phrase like, "Imagine my mother as..." and then do an impression/act-out of a famous person playing your mother.

_____
_____
_____
_____
_____
_____
_____

EXERCISE 44: Creating Observational Jokes

 **Comedy Buddy Exercise**

For the next 3 days, keep track of all the little things you notice about people, places and things. What perplexes you creates great material. Also, things you find that are hard, weird, scary, or stupid.

Put your topics through Stand-up Structure:

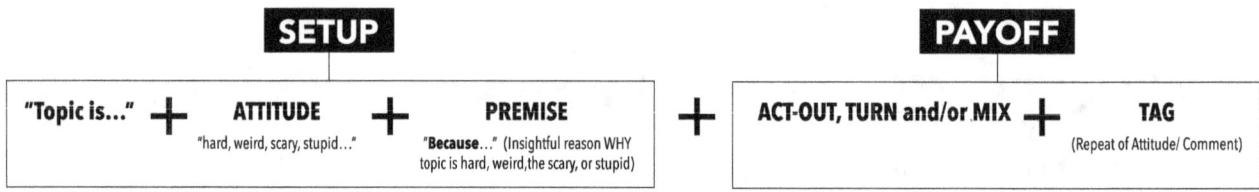

Now, rant and rave with your Comedy Buddy and run through at least 10 observational jokes getting to an act-out, a turn, a dialogue joke, or a comparison. Write them in your Jokes in Progress Section.

EXERCISE 45: Riffing Onstage

With riffing, sometimes an off-handed comment can turn into a chunk. Look up your original jokes and add anything that got laughs to expand your Polished Joke section.

EXERCISE 46: Reluctant Admission

Look through your topics, sub-topics, and micro-topics in Exercises 7 and 8, picking 5 characteristics to exaggerate and turn into a reluctant admission. Write at least 2 versions of the reluctant admission method for each of those 5 characteristics. When finished, move the best material from your exercise folder into your "Jokes in Progress by Topic," and the winners to your "My Act" section.

Characteristic: _____

Lie with confidence and CONVICTION: _____
_____

Admit to the lie with HESITATION: _____
_____

Admit to the lie with EMBARRASSMENT and tell the truth: _____
_____

Say the tag loudly, like "Anyway!" _____

Repeat twice for each of your 5 characteristics:
_____
_____
_____
_____
_____
_____
_____
_____

EXERCISE 47: Terminology Twists

See *The New Comedy Bible* for directions.

TERMS	Act-Out Annoyances and Frustrations
"NETWORKING"	"I'M PRETENDING TO BE INTERESTED SO YOU HIRE ME FOR SOMETHING."

Once you have the list, put each term through this formula:

"You may not know this, but (INSERT TERM) _____
is actually a (INSERT A LANGUAGE, Latin, Yiddish, Farsi, Ancient Egyptian, etc.)
_____ *term, meaning* (FUNNY DEFINITION THAT INCLUDES A MUTUAL FRUSTRATION AND ACT-OUT)_____
_____

Write several of them here:

"You may not know this, but (INSERT TERM) _____
is actually a (INSERT A LANGUAGE, Latin, Yiddish, Farsi, Ancient Egyptian, etc.)
_____ *term, meaning* (FUNNY DEFINITION THAT INCLUDES A MUTUAL FRUSTRATION AND ACT-OUT)_____
_____

"You may not know this, but (INSERT TERM) _____
is actually a (INSERT A LANGUAGE, Latin, Yiddish, Farsi, Ancient Egyptian, etc.)
_____ *term, meaning* (FUNNY DEFINITION THAT INCLUDES A MUTUAL FRUSTRATION AND ACT-OUT)_____
_____

"You may not know this, but (INSERT TERM) _____

is actually a (INSERT A LANGUAGE, Latin, Yiddish, Farsi, Ancient Egyptian, etc.)

_____ *term, meaning* (FUNNY DEFINITION THAT

INCLUDES A MUTUAL FRUSTRATION AND ACT-OUT)_____

_____

EXERCISE 48: Annoying Acronyms

(See *The New Comedy Bible* for instructions.)

Create at least 5 acronyms for existing entities and their "new" meanings:

Acronyms	Annoyances starting with same letters

Input your material into this joke structure:

Did you know that (INSERT ACRONYM) *actually stands for* (INSERT ANNOYANCE WITH SAME LETTERS)?

_____
_____
_____
_____
_____
_____
_____
_____
_____
_____

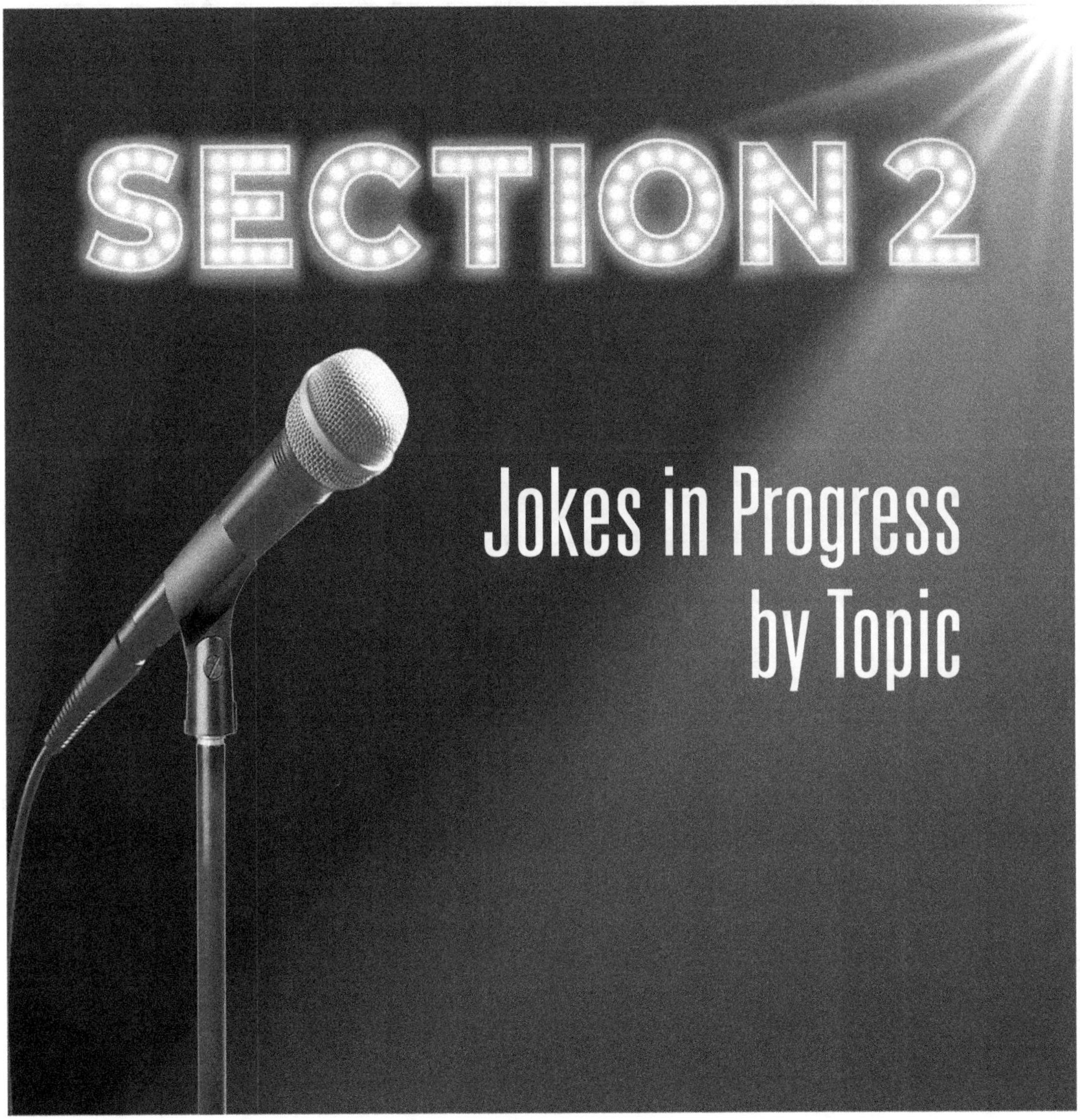

SECTION 2

Jokes in Progress by Topic

This the temporary holding place for your "almost funny" jokes.

Transfer any material you generate from the exercises or from the Morning Writings to this section. When you feel you have a solid joke, copy and paste it to the "My Act" Section.

 "It's not about great writing, it's about the consistency of that writing. I once rewrote a joke for two years before telling it."
— Jerry Seinfeld

Jokes in Progress by Topic
Topic 1 _____

Your Rough Material on this topic:

_____
_____
_____
_____
_____
_____
_____
_____
_____
_____
_____
_____
_____
_____
_____
_____
_____
_____
_____
_____
_____
_____
_____
_____
_____

> "Keep in mind, the more SERIOUS a topic is, the better chance you have of making it funny." — **Judy Carter**

Jokes in Progress by Topic
Topic 2 _____

Your Rough Material on this topic:

> "The best kind of comedy to me is when you make people laugh at things they've never laughed at, and also take a light into the darkened corners of people's minds."
> — **Bill Hicks**

> "Creative freedom is gained when you stop TRYING to be funny and focus on communicating WHY a topic is pisses you off."
> — **Judy Carter**

Jokes in Progress by Topic

Topic 3 _____

Your Rough Material on this topic:

> "When writing premises, don't create just one and then consider yourself done. Write many premises about a topic and when you think you're done, write more." — **Judy Carter**

"The turn has to be LOGICAL. Even though you take the joke in a completely different direction, there must be a connection between where you started and where you end; it has to make sense."
— **Judy Carter**

Jokes in Progress by Topic

Topic 4 _____

Your Rough Material on this topic:

_____
_____
_____
_____
_____
_____
_____
_____
_____
_____
_____
_____
_____
_____
_____
_____
_____
_____
_____
_____
_____
_____
_____
_____
_____

> "Push the topics further than you ever thought you could. Go beyond the expected. That's what makes people laugh — the unexpected."
> — **Judy Carter**

> "Know your audience and build a bridge intersecting YOUR life with THEIRS. Don't talk about your problems UNTIL you connect with the audience by talking about what's bothering THEM." — **Judy Carter**

Jokes in Progress by Topic
Topic 5 _____

Your Rough Material on this topic:

> "Comedy is not about picking funny topics. It's about making ordinary topics funny." — **Judy Carter**

Jokes in Progress by Topic

Topic 6 _____

Your Rough Material on this topic:

"When performing act-outs, face front or angle yourself 45 degrees to the audience. This staging helps differentiate between you and the character you're acting out. Never turn so you're in profile, as that looks amateurish." — **Judy Carter**

> "Whatever a comic talks about onstage is all they talk about offstage." — **Sarah Silverman**

> "Because everyone deals with family issues, doing jokes about your closest relatives is a surefire way to connect with an audience."
> — **Judy Carter**

Jokes in Progress by Topic
Topic 7 _____

Your Rough Material on this topic:

> "Comedians take all of the bad things about themselves and use them to make people laugh." — **Chris Rock**

> "Musicians learn scales. Artists learn composition. Comics need to learn joke structure. It will save you at least 5 years of onstage trial and error." — **Judy Carter**

Jokes in Progress by Topic

Topic 8 _____

Your Rough Material on this topic:

"Use this time in your early career to explore topics that interest you, and play around with various delivery styles. The audience will identify your persona when they connect to an authentic and hilarious vibe in your set." — **Judy Carter**

> "In my workshops, the comic who had no doubts about his or her material, or ability to perform, were often disconnected from themselves. Audiences tend to prefer comics who are authentic and willing to show their vulnerabilities and insecurities." — **Judy Carter**

Jokes in Progress by Topic

Topic 9 _____

Your Rough Material on this topic:

> "The idea that jokes come out of your mouth fully-formed is an expectation guaranteed to ruin your creativity. Tell your inner critic to go f**k themselves." — **Judy Carter**

Jokes in Progress by Topic

Topic 10 _____

Your Rough Material on this topic:

> "I can honestly say, after talking about my mom passing away, I got the biggest weight off my chest. Comedy is my therapy. That's how I deal with my problems, my personal battles. I talk about it. I give it to my fans. When they laugh at it, it's a release." — **Kevin Hart**

> "Some of the best callbacks are those you think of in the moment. When performing, stay open to all possibilities." – **Judy Carter**

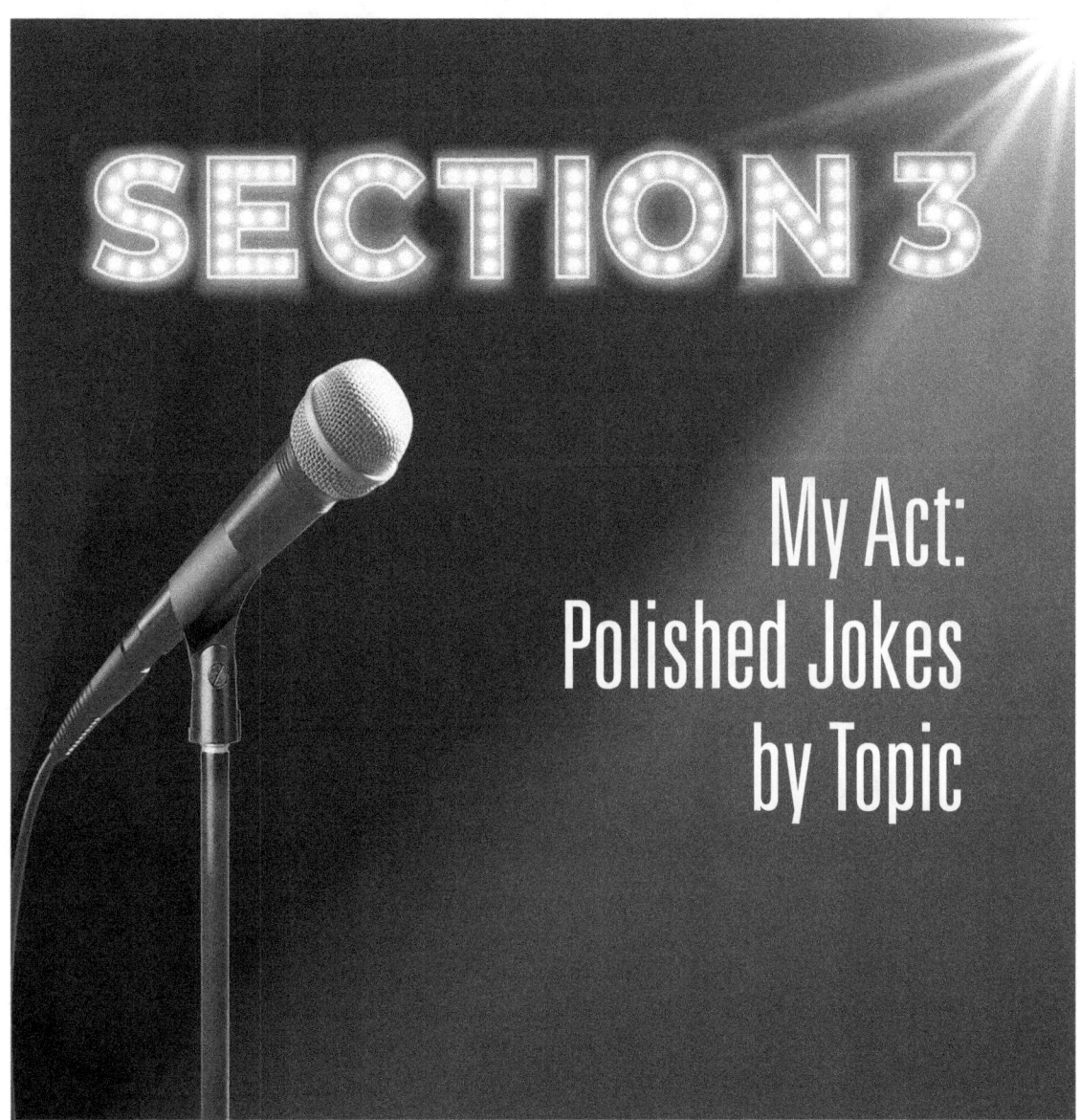

This section contains your polished jokes. They've probably travelled far to get here. Guard this section with your life!

My Act: Polished Jokes by Topic
Topic 1 _____

> "For me, comedy starts as a spew, a kind of explosion, and then you sculpt it from there, if at all. It comes out of a deeper, darker side. Maybe it comes from anger, the hypocrisy that exists everywhere, even within yourself, where it's hardest to see." — **Robin Williams**

My Act: Polished Jokes by Topic

Topic 2 _____

> "Do not practice your jokes on friends. One former student had a great act, then he tried his material out on his buddies. They didn't like it and gave him terrible suggestions. At our class showcase he performed nasty jokes about "blue balls" and totally bombed. Stand-up is not the same thing as telling jokes at a party. Practice with, and trust, your Comedy Buddy." — **Judy Carter**

My Act: Polished Jokes by Topic
Topic 3 _____

> "The first person I learned comedy from said that I should talk about things I am passionate about—that I love or hate—because the audience likes to see passion. The stuff I rant and rave about stems from a place that really pisses me off." — **Lisa Lampanelli**

My Act: Polished Jokes by Topic

Topic 4 _____

> "I don't go, 'I'm gonna write a joke.' I just go through the world and see stuff. It's like I exercise the part of my mind of noticing things to the point where I'm now noticing things without even trying to notice them." — **Stephen Wright**

My Act: Polished Jokes by Topic

Topic 5 _____

> "Comedy writing is something you don't see people doing. It's a secretive thing." — **Jerry Seinfeld**

My Act: Polished Jokes by Topic
Topic 6 _____

> "If attitude is missing from your joke, put one in. You don't have to necessarily say the words, hard, weird, scary, or stupid, but you must convey the feeling of the attitude throughout each joke. The more blatant your attitude, the more laughs you'll get." — **Judy Carter**

My Act: Polished Jokes by Topic

Topic 7 _____

> "Write out a favorite joke word for word, one sentence at a time. After completing each sentence, analyze each word. Why does it work? How do the syllables of the words create rhythm? How do the sentences build to the punchline? What's the grammar of comedy?"
> — Gary Gulman

My Act: Polished Jokes by Topic

Topic 8 _____

> "Your closing is usually your funniest material and often, your most sexual material. So, if you have sexual material, save it for last."
> — **Judy Carter**

My Act: Polished Jokes by Topic
Topic 9 _____

> "Some beginners try to identify their comedy persona BEFORE they've written any jokes. They want to be a 'Trevor Noah type' or a 'Tina Fey type.' What about being a YOU type? After all, that type hasn't been done yet." — **Judy Carter**

My Act: Polished Jokes by Topic
Topic 10 _____

> "If your last bit is 30 seconds, you'll want to perfect transitioning to it from anywhere in your set. Practice going from the middle of your act to the last bit. This technique will prove to be indispensable throughout your career for finishing on time." — **Judy Carter**

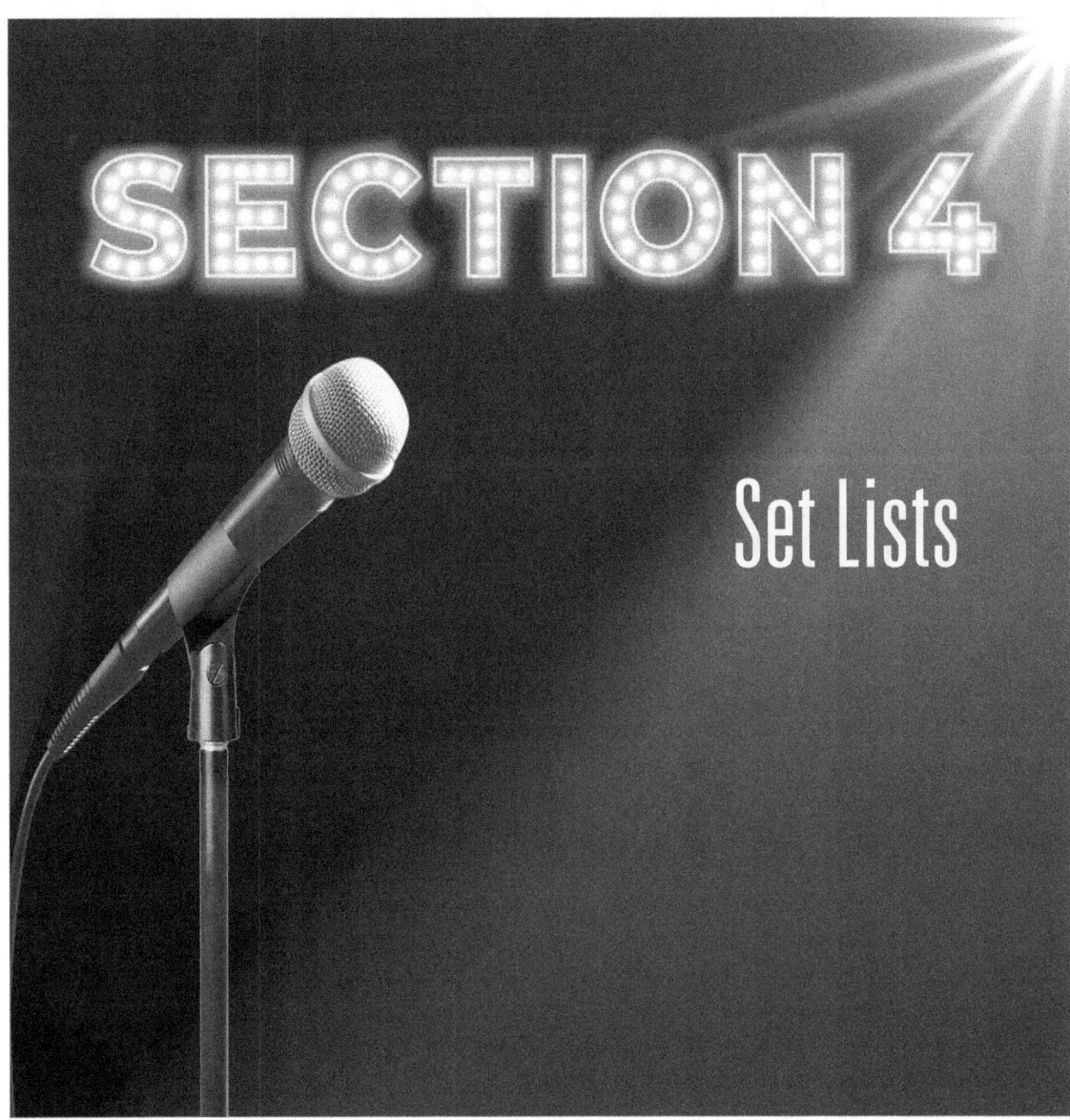

The following is the resting place for your set lists. Organize your material for each engagement depending on the type of audience and how long you're performing.

Set Lists – 3 Minute Set

> 🎤 "Stage time has no substitute. When you fail, get back onstage and try again. Keep what works and lose/rewrite what doesn't. The recipe for success is: Bomb—Try again—Cry—Try again—Eat a pizza—Try again—Repeat! Don't give up!" — **Judy Carter**

Set Lists – 5 Minute Set

 "Stand-up material has to travel. Where you START the joke is not where you END the joke. The TURN is the surprise jump to something that the audience didn't expect. That surprise turn is what makes an audience laugh." — **Judy Carter**

Set Lists – 10 Minute Set

 "The majority of beginning comics think the most important part of a joke is the payoff. Not so. It's the setup. If you don't reel the audience in at the beginning of a joke, they won't be there to laugh at the end."
— Judy Carter

Set Lists - 15 Minute Set

 "When looking down at the set list DURING the laugh, you'll cut it short. It's critical to be 'in the moment' with the audience when they're laughing. Some comics put a drink next to their set list as an excuse to look down." — **Judy Carter**

Set Lists – 30 Minute Set

 "Comedy is a tool of togetherness. It's a way of putting your arm around someone, pointing at something, and saying, 'Isn't it funny that we do that?' It's a way of reaching out." — **Kate McKinnon**

Set Lists - 60 Minute Set

> "DO NOT practice your act in front of a mirror. News flash: In the club, there will be no mirror. The only thing practicing your act in front of a mirror will do is make you more self-conscious. It's best to practice while VISUALIZING an audience, rather than looking at yourself."
> — Judy Carter

Set Lists – Clean Set

> "After delivering the joke's payoff, stay in attitude. Whatever attitude you started the joke with; simply end it with a REPEAT of that attitude." —**Judy Carter**

Set Lists – Themed Events (Women, Late Night, Charity Benefit, Gay Audience, etc.)

Theme: _____

Theme: _____

Theme: _____

Morning Writings

"Nobody can stop you but you. And shame on you if you're the one who stops yourself." — Damon Wayans

The STOP procrastinating system includes:

- A wall calendar (yes, an actual paper monthly calendar on the wall that confronts you every day)
- A red marker (yes, an actual writing instrument so you're interacting with the calendar)
- A notebook (or use your computer, tablet — whatever you're most comfortable with)
- A timer

Then, each morning:

- Set the timer for 10 minutes (you can continue writing after the timer goes off, but DO NOT stop before it goes off).
- Write without stopping, no exceptions, and write everything, even if it's, "I can't think of anything to write."
- Don't try to be funny. Just write anything that comes to your mind.
- **X** out today on your calendar.
- Done

"Jerry Seinfeld told me to get a big wall calendar that has a whole year on one page and hang it on a prominent wall. The next step was to get a big red magic marker. He said for each day that I do my task of writing, I get to put a big red X over that day. After a few days you'll have a chain. Just keep at it and the chain will grow longer and longer. You'll like seeing that chain, especially when you get a few weeks under your belt. Your only job is not to break the chain."
— **Brad Isaac**

Cross off each day you write for at least 10 minutes.

MONTH:_____

SUNDAY	MONDAY	TUESDAY	WEDNESDAY	THURSDAY	FRIDAY	SATURDAY

DON'T BREAK THE CHAIN.

DAY 1 Today's date is: _____

Write whatever comes to mind, or use the writing prompt at the top of each day.

"Someone said something stupid to me, and I wish I'd said..."

DAY 2 Today's date is: _____

"If my clothes could talk, they'd say..."

"Before your coffee, write! Write anything down, including your observations, thoughts, and dreams. This is not high art, but a path to a clearer mind, better ideas and less anxiety." — **Judy Carter**

DAY 3 Today's date is: _____

"If God gave me relationship advice, I'd hear..."

DAY 4 Today's date is: _____

"My first (kiss, relationship, marriage) was weird because…"

"A Comedy Buddy holds you accountable to weekly meetings, doing assignments, and keeping your eye on the prize. Your Comedy Buddy is not only your support system, but they're also the reason you'll get this work done." — **Judy Carter**

DAY 5 Today's date is: _____

"The weirdest things about my parents are..."

> "The basic rule of joking about your family to first establish that you love them. Such as, 'I love my mom... she's great... but a bit crazy...' Only then can you go into their annoyances." — **Judy Carter**

DAY 6   Today's date is: _____

"My opinions have changed. Before, I used to think... but now I think..."

"The hardest thing to do is to be true to yourself, especially when everybody is watching." — **Dave Chappelle**

DAY 7 Today's date is: _____

"The hard things about getting older are…"

"Life opens up opportunities to you, and you either take them or you stay afraid of taking them." — **Jim Carrey**

DAY 8 Today's date is: _____

"The scariest things about my pets are..."

DAY 9 Today's date is: _____

"Can you imagine if I became a parent? It would be like..."

DAY 10 Today's date is: _____

"Dating at my age is hard because..."

"Successful writing comes from perspiration, not inspiration. Don't let your anxiety, a fight with your partner, a bad day at work, or partying the night before take away your commitment to a daily writing schedule. Matter of fact, all those things that used to distract you from writing are MATERIAL." — Judy Carter

DAY 11 Today's date is: _____

"Expectations about best friends are weird because..."

DAY 12 Today's date is: _____

"Current events are scary because..."

"Your comedy persona is being your most authentic self onstage. It's the WAY you tell your jokes." — **Judy Carter**

DAY 13 Today's date is: _____

"Dating/being married is hard because..."

DAY 14 Today's date is: _____

"My body is scary because…"

"I've arrived at the place where if I'm not taking a risk, I'm not happy. If I'm scared, then I know I'm being challenged." — **Jim Carrey**

DAY 15 Today's date is: _____

"It's hard being an adult because..."

DAY 16 Today's date is: _____

"Stereotypes about age are stupid because..."

DAY 17   Today's date is: _____

"The weirdest things about my job are..."

"So many doors can be opened up from stand-up comedy. You can go from acting to being a TV personality to being a radio personality to being a writer to being a producer, to being a visionary, and to voiceover work." — **Kevin Hart**

DAY 18 Today's date is: _____

"It's hard knowing whether to leave or stay because…"

DAY 19 Today's date is: _____

"Vacations are weird because…"

_____
_____
_____
_____
_____
_____
_____
_____
_____
_____
_____
_____
_____
_____
_____
_____
_____
_____
_____
_____
_____
_____
_____
_____
_____
_____
_____
_____

> "Fear of public humiliation is the BEST way to stop procrastinating."
> — Judy Carter

DAY 20   Today's date is: _____

"You know your relationship is over when..."

"Even if you don't want a stand-up comedy career, learning how to write and perform stand-up opens up many job opportunities."
— **Judy Carter**

DAY 21 Today's date is: _____

"It's weird living in (my city) after moving from (other city) because..."

DAY 22 Today's date is: _____

"It was really stupid of me to say..."

> "The most important thing about learning comedy is to start from who you are. If you begin the process by imitating what you perceive to be a comedy rhythm, you will get laughs sooner, but you will not be unique." — **Rita Rudner**

DAY 23   Today's date is: _____

"It's so hard to admit…"

DAY 24 Today's date is: _____

"The hardest thing I had to say to my (spouse, kids, parents) was..."

"People may think I'm trying something new by telling stories, but they're just jokes connected to give the illusion of stories."
— **Steven Wright**

DAY 25 Today's date is: _____

"It's hard to look in the mirror and see..."

DAY 26 Today's date is: _____

"The stupidest fight I've had was about..."

DAY 27 Today's date is: _____

"The scariest things about sex are…"

"Arrange your material the way your body is arranged. Start with your head—do smart stuff about community, family, ethics, heritage, simple observations about life. Then, work your way down to your heart—emotional material about love, heartaches, breakups, and marriage. And end at the groin—sexual material." — **Judy Carter**

DAY 28 Today's date is: _____

"My most memorable failure was..."

DAY 29 Today's date is: _____

"I woke up at 3am and realized..."

"Follow your passion, stay true to yourself, never follow someone else's path. Unless you're in the woods and you're lost and you see a path, then by all means you should follow that." — **Ellen DeGeneres**

DAY 30   Today's date is: _____

"The scariest day of my life was..."

DAY 31 Today's date is: _____

"I made the stupidest mistake when I…"

"As you navigate through the rest of your life, be open to collaboration. Other people's ideas are often better than your own. Find a group of people who challenge and inspire you, spend a lot of time with them, and it will change your life." — **Amy Poehler**

www.ingramcontent.com/pod-product-compliance
Lightning Source LLC
Chambersburg PA
CBHW081153290426

44108CB00018B/2534